Red – Foot Tortoise

A Red – Foot Tortoise Pet Owner's Guide

Red – Foot Tortoise General Info, Purchasing, Care, Cost, Diet, Health, Supplies, and Much More Included!

By: Lolly Brown

Copyrights and Trademarks

All rights reserved. No part of this book may be reproduced or transformed in any form or by any means, graphic, electronic, or mechanical, including photocopying, recording, taping, or by any information storage retrieval system, without the written permission of the author.

This publication is Copyright ©2020 NRB Publishing, an imprint. Nevada. All products, graphics, publications, software and services mentioned and recommended in this publication are protected by trademarks. In such instance, all trademarks & copyright belong to the respective owners. For information consult www.NRBpublishing.com

Disclaimer and Legal Notice

This product is not legal, medical, or accounting advice and should not be interpreted in that manner. You need to do your own due-diligence to determine if the content of this product is right for you. While every attempt has been made to verify the information shared in this publication, neither the author, neither publisher, nor the affiliates assume any responsibility for errors, omissions or contrary interpretation of the subject matter herein. Any perceived slights to any specific person(s) or organization(s) are purely unintentional.

We have no control over the nature, content and availability of the web sites listed in this book. The inclusion of any web site links does not necessarily imply a recommendation or endorse the views expressed within them. We take no responsibility for, and will not be liable for, the websites being temporarily unavailable or being removed from the internet.

The accuracy and completeness of information provided herein and opinions stated herein are not guaranteed or warranted to produce any particular results, and the advice and strategies, contained herein may not be suitable for every individual. Neither the author nor the publisher shall be liable for any loss incurred as a consequence of the use and application, directly or indirectly, of any information presented in this work. This publication is designed to provide information in regard to the subject matter covered.

Neither the author nor the publisher assume any responsibility for any errors or omissions, nor do they represent or warrant that the ideas, information, actions, plans, suggestions contained in this book is in all cases accurate. It is the reader's responsibility to find advice before putting anything written in this book into practice. The information in this book is not intended to serve as legal, medical, or accounting advice.

Foreword

Red – foot tortoises or commonly known as "Red – Foots" are hardy tortoises that are medium in size. They have a docile temperament and generally easy to keep as pets. These tortoises can make ideal pets for first – time owners. The red – footed tortoise is mostly native to different kinds of habitats. In the wild, they can be found in humid tropical forests as well as dry savannahs. Generally, they prefer a more humid setting. Some of them also range in the semi – arid land of South America.

Red – Footed Tortoises particularly hatchlings are usually available in pet trade which are captive – bred species. Adult red – footed tortoises can either come from shelters or breeders but some can also be caught illegally in the wild – something that you don't want to do. Red – foots that are caught in the wild may have acquired certain illnesses and it might not be beneficial to the conservation status of the breed as well.

Red – foots are great South American tortoises to keep as pets. As a potential owner, it is your responsibility to provide for their needs, keep them safe and give them the care they deserve. This book will guide you on how to be the best Red – Foot Tortoise keeper. Enjoy!

Table of Contents

Introduction: Here Comes Red – Foot! 1

Chapter One: Red – Foot Tortoises in Focus 2

    Taxonomy 3

    Color and Size 3

    Red – Foots vs. Yellow - Foots 3

    Species Similar to the Red - Foot Tortoise 4

    Red – Foots in the Wild vs. In Captivity 5

    Can You Keep a Red – Foot? 6

    Conservation Status 8

    Are Red – Foot Tortoises the Ideal Pet For You? 9

    Where Can You Get a Red – Foot Tortoise? 11

    Sources for Your Red – Foot Tortoises 12

    Adopt a Red – Foot Tortoise 13

    Ordering a Tortoise 14

Chapter Two: Red – Foot Tortoises as Pets 20

    Your Companion for Life! 21

    Behavioral Characteristics 22

    Can Red – Foots Get Along with Other Pets? 25

    Things to Consider Before Buying 27

    Health Issues 29

Chapter Three: Red - Foot Essentials 34

Essentials for Hatchling or Juvenile Red - Foots 35

Housing an Adult Red – Foot Tortoise 36

Other Indoor Enclosure Options 37

Enclosure Accessories... 38

Cost of Keeping Red – Foot Tortoises 45

Chapter Four: Health and Wellness 50

Food for Red – Foots... 52

Alfafa Hay vs. Timothy Hay 52

Fruits and Veggies 52

Other Food Options 54

List of Commercial Pellets for Red – Foots 56

Improper Diet May Lead to Health Issues 66

Proper Lighting Requirements.. 68

Health Issues Related to Improper Lighting..................... 70

Chapter Five: Handling and Grooming Red – Foot Tortoises
.... 74

How to Handle a Red – Foot Tortoise............................... 76

Provide a Clean Environment.. 79

Chapter Six: Breeding Season for Red – Foot Tortoises 86

Male or Female? 87

Mating Season 87

Breed Like a Hobbyists 89

Chapter Seven: Maintenance Tips for Red – Foot Tortoises 92

    Building a Tortoise Pen 93

    Play Pen for Your Red - foot 94

    Tortoise Ratio 96

    Secure Your Pet Red - foot 97

Index 100

    Glossary 104

Photo Credits 110

References 112

Introduction: Here Comes Red – Foot!

What are red – foot tortoises? We will give you a brief description of what red – foot tortoises are in terms of their physical appearance. In the next few chapters, you'll learn more about their behaviors, habitat needs, diet, and the likes. For now, let's get you familiar with this interesting tortoise breed.

Your hatchling tortoise will eventually mature into adulthood. You can expect their carapaces (shell) to have a more elongated oval shape with almost parallel sides. Their shells are highly domed and also smooth. Their hips area has a high – point that's followed by a sloped region that's

Introduction: Here Comes Red – Foot!

near their neck. They have either dark brown colored costal and vertebral scutes, or a black one. You can see some marginals along the sides of their body which is flaring just a little over their limbs. In the middle of the lower edge, they usually exhibit a dark color.

As they become bigger, you may notice their growth rings grow as well. However, these rings may not be visibly clear. The plastron has thick edges that are also large. Their gulars don't past the front are of their carapace.

They have a small head with a flat top. Their eyes are generally large with black – colored iris.

The red – foot tortoise is an interesting breed that has a hooked upper jaw. It's jagged in the middle and you can notice that they have tiny groves on each side. Tortoises generally have a tympanum, and for red – foots these are found just below the eye. There are also irregular, small scales on their head along with the scales that's found on their body; the color of their scales range from yellowish to brick – red shade.

Introduction: Here Comes Red – Foot!

The shape of their limbs is cylindrical with four claws on their forelegs, and five on their hind legs. What a lot of people don't know is that they may be called as "red – foots" but they don't have visible toes. Their forelegs are flat in a way while their front surface has large scales. The scales have the same color as their head. Finally, when it comes to their tails, the length of it varies. It's generally muscular, and it does not have any claw on the tip.

On the next chapter, we'll give you an overview of how they are as household pets. Read on!

Introduction: Here Comes Red – Foot!

Chapter One: Red – Foot Tortoises in Focus

Red – foots are popular household tortoise pets and that's mainly because of their striking shell coloring. Like most turtle and tortoise species, they are generally easy to maintain and can live for a long time. They sort of have that stereotypical – look for a tortoise. Red – foot tortoises have a large shell that has interesting marking on the top. If you are thinking of keeping a red – footed tortoise as a pet, keep in mind that even if they are not high – maintenance pets, they live way longer than a conventional household pet. Just make sure that you are prepared to keep them for the long run before you make a commitment or acquire them.

Chapter One: Red – Foot Tortoises in Focus

Taxonomy

The red – foot tortoise belong to Class *Reptilia*, Order *Chelonia/ Testudines*, Family *Testudinidae*, Species *Chelonoidis carbonaria*.

Color and Size

Red – footed tortoises have a high domed shell with red to yellow – orange marking on the face. They typically have orange – red scales to yellow – reddish shade on their forelimbs. Each keratin scute on their carapace (upper shell) typically has a yellow - colored center. The sizes of a typical adult red – foot tortoise usually vary but it can measure around 30 to 50 cm or 12 to 20 inches.

Red – Foots vs. Yellow - Foots

The easiest way on how breeders identify a red – foot tortoise from a yellow – foot tortoise is through the scales on their head. Yellow – foots usually have longer scales on the top of their head near their nose area. These are known as pre – frontal scales.

Chapter One: Red – Foot Tortoises in Focus

They also sport a fragmented frontal scale which can be found in the front area of the pre – frontal scales. On the other hand, red – foots have shorter pre – frontal scales but a more visible frontal scale.

Aside from the difference in scales, female red – foot breeds usually have a more elongated body shape while adult male red – foots have hourglass shape.

On the other hand, male and female yellow – footed tortoises have a rounder and flatter overall body shape. Red – footed and yellow – footed males can be identified from females because they generally have longer tail and concave plastron.

Species Similar to the Red - Foot Tortoise

If you want to know similar – looking breeds, you can check out these other tortoises:

- Hermann's Tortoises
- Indian Star Tortoise
- Leopard Tortoise

Chapter One: Red – Foot Tortoises in Focus

Red – Foots in the Wild vs. In Captivity

Wild red – footed species, who are prolific diggers, are mostly found in the regions of South America. They typically burrow so that they can have a safe shelter to stay in especially when the temperature becomes to humid for them, and if they need to hide from any predator. Most tortoises find it comforting to hide in a spot where they can tightly fit in. This is why they are often found inside a tree trunk, sometimes with fellow tortoises.

Red – foot tortoises also display social behavior in the wild. They often hang out with their fellow species, sharing food together and just gathering in small groups like how it is in a pack. Compare to other turtle/ tortoise species, they are not overly territorial particularly when it comes to nesting or during feeding time. The only time that they will compete with one another is when two males are competing on who will get to mate with a female during breeding season.

In captivity, red – foot tortoises may often be shy to interact or wander around the terrarium. You may find themselves burrowing or hiding especially when they feel

Chapter One: Red – Foot Tortoises in Focus

stressed out. Most turtles and tortoises in general don't want to be handled. This is why you have to ensure that you prevent young kids from handling them because not only will it stress the tortoise, kids can also be infected with salmonella.

Can You Keep a Red – Foot?

Are you legally allowed to keep a red - foot tortoise? Well, there are varying degrees in which legal protection is afforded to red - foot tortoises but due to continuous illegal capture in certain areas it can still be a threat to this species.

You won't really need to get a license if you decide to keep or breed these adorable creatures because they are listed in the Appendix Two of the Convention on International Trade in Endangered Species which means that they can be traded for commercial purposes but they can't be taken from the wild unless you got the approval of wildlife organizations or authorities.

Since tortoises like red - foots falls under the Appendix Two category it also implies that you will not be allowed to transport these tortoises from one country to another if you don't have an export certificate from wildlife organizations and from your country of origin. You'll also need to secure an import certificate to the country of your destination.

If you want to travel or transport your pet tortoise, you should have these certificates in order to satisfy authorities that your pet is obtained legally. It may vary from one state or country to another but authorities may need to check document that states the name and identity of your red - foot tortoises.

You'll also need to state your name address, contact details as well as other personal information to be kept for future reference and also for legality purposes. If as a keeper or breeder you don't comply with the regulations, authorities has grounds to automatically confiscate your pet tortoises, pay a fine, and even face imprisonment. If you're going to buy or sell red - foot tortoises from other countries, you'll need an authorization for import to make sure that they will be legally imported.

Chapter One: Red – Foot Tortoises in Focus

Tortoises being traded in other countries sometimes can be hard for authorities to differentiate whether or not they are wild or captive – bred specimens which sometimes contribute to illegal importation.

Conservation Status

In many South American countries, red - foot tortoises are more than just pets, they are symbols of longevity, happiness and fertility which is why conservation activities are much easier to promote and maintain. Smuggling of these tortoises in South American countries is evident because enforcement is insufficient which is why wildlife advocates are aiming to address this problem. The good thing is that these red - foot tortoises thrives in captivity and breeds easily in countries like United States making it enough to supply the demand for these pets.

The illegal pet trade paved way for environmental organizations established a program in South American countries on how to protect illegal smuggling of pet tortoises. They've also established an information, breeding and protection center and even initiated some conservation projects to further protect these species, which is why despite of the continuous desertification threat in the country, there are still a lot of people who are willing to preserve these wildlife gems.

In other countries where red - foot tortoises are native and previously abundant are increasingly declining in terms of population because of natural habitat loss due to domestic livestock and continuous urbanization.

Are Red – Foot Tortoises the Ideal Pet For You?

You should only keep a red – foot tortoise if you prefer a docile, quiet and non – threatening creature that doesn't require any training or socialization. Generally speaking, it requires no supervision, provided that its enclosure is safe and secured. Keeping them is not that costly and not hard to maintain during its early years

Red – foot tortoises are suited for expert keepers and beginners alike. They are mostly available in local pet shops or reptile conventions. They are generally very easy to feed;

Chapter One: Red – Foot Tortoises in Focus

they are vegetarian and commercial foods are also available in reptile shops or major pet stores. They are unlikely to get ill with appropriate care and also don't shed and doesn't need to be groomed. Overall, red – foot tortoises are very fun to keep and easy to raise especially when they're still hatchlings or juveniles.

A red – foot tortoise is not for you if you're not ready to keep a pet for more than 20 years. Growth may be relatively hard to manage since they can get huge and heavier over time. Costs for food, caging and other materials when they reach adulthood could become relatively expensive.

They are not an ideal pet if you only live in a small house because it needs lots of space as it grows; this pet is ideal for keepers who have a backyard. They may need supervision once it reaches adulthood. Keeping more than one tortoise can be harder to maintain in the long run and also time consuming

Chapter One: Red – Foot Tortoises in Focus

If you become a breeder of these species, you need to make sure that you can take care of all the hatchlings as they grow up because it's hard to find rescue centers, put them up for adoption or even give them to people if you won't be able to handle their needs one day.

Where Can You Get a Red – Foot Tortoise?

It's essential that before you purchase a red – foot tortoise, you should first consider on who bred and raised them. Keep in mind that purchasing a healthy breed is one of the most essential things that every potential reptile keeper should learn about. In this section you will be provided with the criteria on selecting a healthy red – foot tortoise and be given criteria to spot a reputable and trustworthy breeder. You will also learn where to legally purchase tortoises. You'll also be provided with links to possibly legit breeders and rescue centers.

Chapter One: Red – Foot Tortoises in Focus

Sources for Your Red – Foot Tortoises

Before comparing the benefits of adopting tortoises from rescue centers and purchasing from hobbyists or legit breeders, it's probably best to first address why buying from pet stores is somewhat discouraged. We all know that pet shops are the go – to place when it comes to purchasing different kinds of animals like red - foot tortoises but the main downside in buying from such pet stores especially those that are not locally recognized shops is that there's a nine of ten instances that these local pet shops don't really care about the pets that they sell.

Based from many experienced keepers, these pet shops are only selling pets for the money. Of course, it's still a business but the thing is that you can't be assured of the pet's health. I'm not saying that all local pet shops are selling unhealthy breeds but most of the time they don't really care for this pets which should be your top most concerned as a potential keeper.

Chapter One: Red – Foot Tortoises in Focus

You would want to acquire a species that is a product of good breeding practices to ensure that they are not sick or doesn't carry other diseases which could affect your collection (if you have one) and to also ensure that they are not illegally obtained.

Pet stores housing red - foot tortoises with other exotic animals from other countries is also to be avoided as these exotic animals could be carriers of diseases which could be passed on to the tortoise. Bottom line is that, as much as possible, acquire a pet tortoise from rescue centers, from legit breeders or even hobbyists found in reptile conventions because it eliminates lots of risks in terms of breeding and husbandry in the long run since legit breeders are passionate about raising such animals.

Adopt a Red – Foot Tortoise

In terms of adopting adult and even hatchling red - foot tortoises, you can have a hard time finding them because there are some rescue centers that doesn't cater to tortoises or other reptile species since these creatures gets bigger; these centers obviously cannot provide enough

Chapter One: Red – Foot Tortoises in Focus

housing space. There could be pet shelters and a rescue center that accommodates red - foot tortoises but that depends on your location.

The reasons why these adorable creatures end up in rescues is because they could have escaped its confines or most of the time an overwhelmed hobbyist may have bitten off more than what one could chew and couldn't take care of the pet properly.

Adopting from rescues is not only a good way to give the tortoise a new loving keeper, but it also discourages the purchase of hatchlings from indiscriminate tortoise breeders who are only out to make a quick buck.

The best part is that if you have found a healthy and sweet looking red - foot from one of these rescue centers, they could be much cheaper to buy compared to acquiring one from a hobbyist or a legit breeder.

Ordering a Tortoise

The packaging is very important if you're going to order a red – foot tortoise. This is because you need to make sure that the animals are well protected. Make sure that your

Chapter One: Red – Foot Tortoises in Focus

breeder/ source is partnered up with other businesses that shipped reptiles so that you can get the lowest rate possible.

If you're going to ship tortoises, the first step is to prepare a box or a normal size cube that measures around 10 x 10 inches. Make sure that the box is quite thick and made up of quality cardboards. Don't forget to print out a sign that says "perishable goods" or "handle with care" and put some arrows in it in red font color so that the delivery man will take care of it during delivery.

The next step is to cut out or buy a Styrofoam that's the same size and shape of your box. The foam inserts has two functions, the first one is that they cushion the package inside and the second one is it insulates the animal from outside temperatures, so that you or your customers won't have to worry about the tortoise getting too cold or whatnot. Just slide the foams on all sides of the box, make sure that they're exactly fitted in the box's size.

After setting up the box, you can buy plastic cups that look like a water dish or sort of a shallow bowl (not the glass cups, more of a delicups). Once you do, just go ahead and put air holes in it using a tool to poke through the cup.

Make a couple of air holes on the plastic cup but not on the box or the foam otherwise it will defeat the purpose of the foam's insulation capabilities because it will let the outside air get inside the box and could make your tortoise uncomfortable during its shipment. You can assure your customers by explaining to them that unlike mammals or humans, tortoises don't breathe as much as we do since they are cold – blooded creatures, so they won't have to worry about the animal not getting enough air inside the box or becoming suffocated because the foams are not air tight, it's only insulated.

Once you've prepared the cup, just tear out a newspaper and crumple it, then put it inside the cup because it will serve as the temporary bedding of the baby tortoise. After doing that, you can go ahead and pick out which baby tortoise is going to go.

Chapter One: Red – Foot Tortoises in Focus

Before you do, however, make sure to give them a quick look. Make sure that the tortoise is responsive, has bright and clear eyes, and free of any discharge. Behaviorally speaking, they should be quite scared when getting picked up since they're still babies, they could sort of pull back into their shells – that's actually a good sign that you've properly nursed them.

Make sure that the tortoises are also soaked or hydrated before packing them up because you just never know how long the shipment could take or whatnot, this is just to prepare them for a trip before reaching their new homes. Usually, depending on how far you're going to deliver them, these tortoises are going to be spending around 2 days or more but you don't have to worry about that since they pretty much naturally stay underground as hatchlings.

Once you've checked them out and prepped them up, you can then place them inside the cup, put the lid and close it. After that, place the cup inside the box then just take a couple more shreds of newspapers, crumple them up and

Chapter One: Red – Foot Tortoises in Focus

place it in the four corners with the cup being the center to prevent it from getting swayed on either sides of the box.

Take a couple more crumpled newspapers and put them on top to provide added security. You can include whatever you want like before you sealed the box, just place some instructions, reminders, a thank you note or some kind of surprise for your customer. You also have to attach a small packaged size heat pad inside the insulated roof (insert it inside the box before completely closing it) to keep the tortoise warm as well.

Once it's all done, just insert the top piece of foam and close the box using a packaging tape to completely seal it. The packaging doesn't have to be pretty but it has to be secure.

Before shipping a tortoise, make sure that you do your research about the particular species because obviously the instructions provided here may only be applicable to grassland tortoises in general like the red – foot tortoises since these species are not aquatic or semi – aquatic like the turtles. Try to also read or research the laws regarding

Chapter One: Red – Foot Tortoises in Focus

shipping or selling particular tortoise or turtle species because some breeds could be prohibited in being delivered.

Chapter Two: Red – Foot Tortoises as Pets

Before getting yourself into a situation which may later surprise or worse alarm you, you should keep in mind the practicality of keeping red – foot tortoise as pets. The main difference between a tortoise and a turtle is that the former are terrestrial type of creatures while the latter are mostly semi – aquatic animals. Compared to turtles, tortoises tend to get much bigger, heavier and most species live longer than turtles.

Chapter Two: Red – Foot Tortoises as Pets

Tortoises and turtles alike are believed to be one of the oldest animal species on earth. Their ancestors go as far back around the time of the dinosaurs and some researchers also believe that they are perhaps the longest living species that survived to this day without evolving much and doesn't have any significant change in terms of their physical characteristics. In this chapter, you'll learn more about how to deal with them as pets, and a basic overview of what to expect.

Your Companion for Life!

Nope, I'm not exaggerating! As mentioned in the previous chapter, tortoises on average can live for more than 30 or 40 years. This is the same for red – foot tortoises. These tiny and adorable creatures will grow fast and will require a lot of your attention and time. Not only will you have to consider the size it can grow to, you will also need to consider the available space you have at home. Make sure that you are ready for some very long term commitment because this species can probably outlive you.

Chapter Two: Red – Foot Tortoises as Pets

Point of No Return

If after a couple of years, you're already bored with your pet tortoise, keep in mind that it is illegal to release a tortoise back in the wild. If an individual is caught, one could be heavily fined, so if you become overwhelmed by the baby red - foot tortoises that you bought or produced, you will have to do what is right by researching and looking for ways to correctly disperse them, and not just throw them away. Think about how many you can handle up to the time that they grow larger before buying a lot of this. In fact, I highly recommend you to just start with one.

Behavioral Characteristics

Red – foot tortoises like most tortoise species are gentle and docile pets. They are perhaps one of the least threatening animals in the world both in captivity and in the wild. As we all know they just hide inside their tough hard shells if they are being threatened by predators in the wild which is perhaps the best defensive strategy. They literally carry their own shelter wherever they go which makes them live longer and feel secure even if they don't possess any

Chapter Two: Red – Foot Tortoises as Pets

significant striking or offensive skills compared to other reptiles or animals. They are very hardy tortoises which is part of the reason why they are so popular. These cute little bunches are very active, they start eating right away, and they also possess an amazing shell color compared to other tortoises or turtles.

Natural Diggers

In the wild and even in captivity, red - foot tortoises love to hide and dig large burrows just to get away from the extreme heat of the sun especially for those tortoises living in dryer areas and harsh environments in South America where most red – foot tortoises are found. Red - foot tortoises are natural diggers, and in the wild, they are very important creatures because since they're the ones who can dig deep holes, other animals tend to share in that shading if they can't come out because it's too hot. Other animals like snakes, monitor lizards, iguanas and other reptiles help one another in a way and even live in the bottom part of the burrows that's about 60 feet deep. Most tortoises spend both cold and hot days under these burrows.

Chapter Two: Red – Foot Tortoises as Pets

Red - foot tortoises are prefer humid and dry environments, but that doesn't mean that you won't provide them water or a cooling area. You will learn more about how to set up an enclosure for your tortoises in the next few chapters.

Since they are naturally adapted to a hotter temperature, they have found a way on how to survive despite the harsh conditions by only coming out if the temperature in the desert is just right which is usually around the dawn and dusk hours. Nocturnal animals are those that are active at night while diurnal animals are those that are active during the day, but most tortoises including red – foots fall under the category of corpuscular which are species that are neither nocturnal or diurnal because most of the time they're just staying under the burrow that they dug up using their huge claws waiting for the right time and perfect temperature to come out and explore the outside world.

Chapter Two: Red – Foot Tortoises as Pets

Can Red – Foots Get Along with Other Pets?

Well, if you have a normal household pet like a dog or cat, you definitely don't want to mingle them all together. Red – foot tortoises are even-tempered reptiles that could share space only with its kind and a few other turtle or younger tortoise species given that they are provided enough room to be housed comfortably.

Many hobbyists aim to integrate many of their reptile pets in one habitat and though this is possible and often successfully accomplished by experienced keepers, tanks housing mixed - species of turtles or reptiles can be very challenging to keep clean, is quite costly and can also be time consuming.

Don't House Them All in One Space

Although red - foot tortoises are docile and seemingly non – threatening to humans, they can show aggressiveness towards other tortoise species especially when its territory is threatened or if food is not enough within the enclosure because it can obviously create a competition.

Chapter Two: Red – Foot Tortoises as Pets

It can possibly show its innate rage and prey upon other species if it is housed with other tortoises but as long as you provide them with more than enough space as they grow and give them a fair amount of food and other necessities to live a comfortable captive life, then you won't have a problem with housing them in one habitat. If you are planning to house multiple species or red - foot tortoises in one tank you will need to follow a thought out strategy to help them be comfortable with one another.

You may need to provide a lot of extra space with many hiding places and visible barriers. You also have to ensure that all species are fed separately to make sure that each one is properly fed.

No socialization or interaction is needed prior to mixing them with other tortoise species because they can pretty much get along, however if you may need to quarantine new species to prevent the spread of possible illnesses particularly Salmonella bacteria.

Chapter Two: Red – Foot Tortoises as Pets

Things to Consider Before Buying

It is quite challenging to identify a reputable reptile breeder. These are common when tortoises are bred in captivity. So it will still be largely up to you to research and seek out the best breeders who are open to answering questions about the origins of the tortoise, the methods employed during production and hatch period as well as other important husbandry practices he/she have done. If a breeder lets you walk - through in their facilities to see the conditions and living environment of the animals housed within their site, that's a great indicator of a legit breeder; all these could indicate a breeder who aims to follow the protocol for breeding these tortoises.

Stay away from super discounted red – foot tortoise traders since the discount itself could be a giveaway of an abundance of pets resulting to slashed prices in order to get rid of excess hatchlings. After determining your reputable breeder, and assessing your financial capabilities, you will have to conduct a very simple physical exam to ensure that the species you will get is worth the investment.

Chapter Two: Red – Foot Tortoises as Pets

Red - foot tortoises should be alert, active and inquisitive. They should not appear lethargic and if you give them food, they should at least have an appetite for it. Pick up the tortoise and determine whether it weighs heavy or light because a light turtle may be ill.

The next test is to gently tug at one of its legs. The reaction of an ill tortoise will be slow and less vigorous whereas a healthy tortoise will be quick to react strongly. You should also scrutinize the top and bottom halves of its shell. They should be sandy or smooth, hard and has yellowish or light brown shaded plates. If the shell is soft once you touch it, this could indicate shell rot. Take note of the occurrence of open wounds, discharge from eyes and their interaction with other pets.

Going to a reptile pet shop or rescue center is convenient but going online to buy your red - foot tortoise will save you some money. If you want to see your chosen tortoise up close and personal, however, you may want to opt for local breeders in your area, speak to other red – foot breeders or try looking for reptile online groups. The people in these groups are usually knowledgeable about reptiles and tortoises in general, and may give you good advice on where to acquire a red – foot tortoise.

Health Issues

One of the most common health issues of tortoises is a tortoise prolapsed. The small opening sometimes called cloacae in a tortoise's scute just under its tail leading to the animal's reproductive system, the rectal area and the bladder is where prolapsed can take place. Prolapsed are when the tissues or some part of internal organs comes out through the tortoise's opening.

Unlike most mammals that have water – soluble urea, when these tortoises expel uric acid in the form of urine, it is not water – soluble. It can often time appear as a diluted or concentrated white urine. When this concentrated urea pass through the animal's kidney and the tortoise is always dehydrated or is in a poor diet, this uric acid can become a hard stone in the bladder. Once the body pushes the large and hard stone from the abdominal muscles to the cloacae, it can go up against the soft organs or tissues and instead of the stone being pushed out, the organs, like a male's tortoise's phallus is pushed out instead this is what you call prolapsed.

This often time happens among male tortoises, their phallus or penis is where sperm pass through during copulation, so if the phallus is exposed and becomes damaged or dry it won't be able to retract itself back into the shell or the body. When this happens, take your tortoise to the vet as soon as possible.

Vets will try to carefully push the organ inside by applying a hypertonic solution similar to dextrose to draw out the fluid in the swollen penis and shrink it. After that, the phallus will be lubricated and gently be pushed back inside. Vets will then place a suture in the skin of the external opening to stop the organ from coming out until the animal recovers. It will usually take a week or so to fully recover before the sutures are completely removed.

Chapter Two: Red – Foot Tortoises as Pets

If you bring your pet to the vet as early as you can, it will be much easier to push the organ back to its cloacae but if you don't and the organ becomes too dry, the procedure may not be successful and the phallus could be amputated – which means that the tortoise won't be able to reproduce anymore. Other procedures involve a surgery in the bottom shell of the tortoise to remove the large stones that formed in the bladder; this procedure however, can be very expensive and complicated. Small stones are often treatable through proper hydration so that it can eventually be soluble.

Prolepses can sometimes be caused through mating, because the phallus of the male tortoises are bruised, so make sure to routinely check them every now and then especially if they are housed with female tortoises so that you can separate them to prevent continuous damage to the organ.

Another common issue is eye syndrome. One of the more preventable and easily treatable illnesses observed in a tortoise is the eye syndrome. This condition is largely due to improper lighting, hygiene and diet. This is almost always caused by a lack of vitamin A and vitamin D, both of which the animal can get from a proper diet and proper lighting of its habitat.

Chapter Two: Red – Foot Tortoises as Pets

Chapter Three: Red - Foot Essentials

One of the most important things that pets need in general is a suitable environment to live in. As the potential owner, you need to ensure that they are well – housed in an environment that feels like their natural habitat in the wild. You have to prepare an ample space in your house where they can roam around as they get older and set up a terrarium with all the basic necessities they need in order to grow happy and healthy. In this chapter, you'll learn the housing requirements suited for hatching or juvenile red - foot tortoises.

Chapter Three: Red - Foot Essentials

We'll discuss on the basic essentials they need and you'll also learn the reason why these factors can contribute to making your pet feel safe and comfortable. We will also cover the estimated cost that red – foot tortoise keeping will entail.

Essentials for Hatchling or Juvenile Red - Foots

You have to compare your young red - foot tortoise with a real life baby. They're like little toddlers walking around and investigating things, they're curious and they basically wanted to learn how to get along with other species and deal with life. With that being said you have to ensure that the habitat you set up will provide their environmental needs and is not dangerous for them. If you have a collection of other tortoise species, there'll be times that you see them flipping over lying in the back of their shells just like toddlers, so you have to also ensure that all the ornaments or cage decorations you place inside the enclosure are easy enough for them to get in and out of.

Chapter Three: Red - Foot Essentials

Housing an Adult Red – Foot Tortoise

When it comes to housing a full – grown red – foot tortoise, you have to keep in mind that they like to be in a solid structure where they can't see through.

Compared to turtles, tortoises will totally spend their time pacing the glass so it's important that you put them in an enclosure or tank where they cannot see through. If you want other people to easily view your pet or if you're going to buy a glass terrarium, it's probably better if you black out the rest of the enclosure's sides and only leave one clear side of the glass.

DIY Tortoise Tables

This is the reason why a wooden tortoise table is ideal especially for land dwellers like the red - foot tortoises, you can search online for tortoise table ideas and you can even buy and assemble a wooden enclosure from pet stores. If you're sort of a craftsman, you can try creating your own tortoise table and a DIY terrarium. This can help save you a few bucks and you can create it in a specification of your choice.

Other Indoor Enclosure Options

Wooden Bookshelves

Another option is to turn old wooden bookshelves. Just clean them up, turn them on the side and make sure that the bottom part is strong and intact because that's obviously where you will put all the substrate and cage materials for your tortoise. Ensure that it doesn't fall off or have any holes where your baby tortoises can sneak through. If you do that you can easily save money and time rather than building one yourself.

Plastic Tubs

If you don't prefer wooden enclosures, but still want to save money or you don't have the time to shop for terrariums, you can easily purchase a cheap wide plastic tub or mixing tubs, preferably not the clear ones, from your local home depot. These tubs can be a perfect alternative for glass terrariums because they are open.

Chapter Three: Red - Foot Essentials

The major advantage of these open tubs because you can easily lift it up, its light since it's made out of plastic and you can easily place it outside your house so that your baby tortoises can get some natural sunlight, though you may need to put a screen to keep them safe from birds or other predators.

Make sure to also remove it if the weather becomes bad outside. Tubs are suitable nursing enclosures for hatchlings at least for the next 6 months.

Enclosure Accessories

Substrate

You should opt to purchase Reptibar type of substrate because it can stay dry. You can also take organic potting soil and mix it together to create a substrate. Reptibar substrate is not something that your red - foot tortoise will nibble on so you don't have to worry about impaction, just make sure that you don't mist it since most tortoises likes dryer surface. It's also easy to spot clean because you can easily scoop your pet's poop. It's also very neat looking.

Sphagnum Moss

If tortoises are not provided with a humid hiding area it tends to make their shells go much rougher. What you can do is to provide a humid hiding spot where they can bask or burrow. You should provide them with sphagnum moss which is something that you can buy in a pet store or something that is placed for indoor plants.

What you should do is to soak the sphagnum moss in some water, squeeze out the excess water, and place it underneath the hiding area or cave. This will provide a humid area that your tortoise can enjoy.

(Humid) Hiding Area

When it comes to purchasing a hiding area, you can choose from several designs found in pet shops, just make sure to adjust the size as your tortoise gets bigger over time. If you're in a tight budget, what you can do is to get a boot of a tree or some sort of log where your red - foot turtles can go under, don't forget to put the moist sphagnum moss inside so that you can make a realistic replica of their natural environment.

Just put it all there and allow the animal to seek it out within the enclosure, they will pretty much use it to bask or nestle in which is perfect for their overall shell covering.

Basking Equipment

Basking your red - foot tortoise is very important for the development of its shell so make sure that you provide them with the lights and heat they need for them to have basking options within their enclosure.

You can choose from different kinds of basking light since there are lots of products out there that provide bright lights which could help your tortoise and fit inside your enclosure.

Heating and Lighting Options

There are different types of heating equipment including a ceramic heater which could provide a lot more heat and could easily heat up a larger space or big enclosures; another one is called halogen bulbs which are good to develop your pet's shell. You can also purchase a rheostat because it can also aid in regulating lighting temperature inside the enclosure.

Chapter Three: Red - Foot Essentials

One of the basking options is called a ceramic heater this kind of heating equipment will obviously not give off any light because it only provides nothing but pure heat, this may not be suitable if your enclosure is a Rubbermaid tub. It works best for tanks or glass terrariums. Ceramic heaters are lasts for a long time and can be beneficial because red – foots prefers a humid surrounding.

The next option for basking is halogen bulbs; this kind of equipment is could be very hot and very bright for your pet tortoise. This is also suitable for hatchling red – foots tortoises because it's safer.

If you purchase a low wattage bulb, you can just have two or three of it, and put it over a section of the cage providing your pet with a basking zone. The downside is that halogen bulbs tend to break easily if it is moved too much.

However, buying two or three of these halogen bulbs is better than just purchasing one thick bulb; this is because a thick bulb can create a hot spot or even burn your pet whereas the three bulb spread across a portion of the enclosure is much more ideal in providing the needed temperature in the basking area.

Chapter Three: Red - Foot Essentials

Your pet will also need UVB bulb. It's very important equipment for basking especially if you won't have the time to expose them under the sun every morning. These bulbs will simulate the sun's heat.

After purchasing those lights and heating equipment, you can have two options when it comes to its set up. The first is that you can choose to buy a lighting bulb and UVB bulb and attached it to a fixture located on one side of the enclosure so that your pet can have an area where they can bask in. The second option is for you to buy a single lamp that will provide lighting through the entire enclosure then attached the same UVB bulb in your fixture and place it on one side so that your pet tortoise can have both options available – the light and the heat.

Water Dish

The first thing a hatchling tortoise need is water. It doesn't matter if a tortoise is from a desert or a jungle; you have to make sure that you provide with clean water for your young red – foot tortoises.

Chapter Three: Red - Foot Essentials

It's highly recommended that you purchase shallow water bowls because if you buy water dishes that are deep or big enough for their size, they can accidentally flip over and if you don't notice them they can definitely die since they're not aquatic species like turtles.

Don't fill up the water bowl too deep, just place an amount where they can easily put their heads under to drink and a dish that they can get out of, if in case they flip on their backs to avoid drowning.

Food Dish

You can buy different kinds of food dish that comes in many sizes and colors from pet stores or you can save money by purchasing a flower pot dish made out of clay.

You can easily get it at hardware stores or local home centers for a very cheap price. You have to keep in mind that, just like the water dish, the food dish or bowl is also shallow where your hatchling red – foot tortoise can conveniently access.

Chapter Three: Red - Foot Essentials

The advantage of using a clay or rough type of food dish is that it could develop your tortoise beak or mouth because as it eats in the dish, it can naturally scratch off its excess beak. If you use plastic or stainless food dishes, it can cause problems because they are not being fed on something hard which can cause problems since their beak will become too long or overgrown. If this happens you might need to use some trimming device to cut off the excess beak which can be quite an unpleasant experience for your hatchling red – foot pets.

Misting Duties

Just do a light misting once or twice a day to replicate dew in the morning or the moist they experience in their natural surroundings. Even if red – foot tortoises are from deserts, it's important that they stay hydrated.

Soaking Dish

This is optional if you want to soak your red – foot tortoise, you can do these at thrice a week especially if you live in a warmer location.

Chapter Three: Red - Foot Essentials

Just fill it up with a bit of water and let them soak there for about 10 minutes. If you want to know if you're tortoise is sufficiently hydrated, once you soak it sometimes they will expel a white toothpaste gooey looking substance on their rear end, don't be worried because that's actually an indicator that they are hydrated.

If you see this white stuff in a more powder form, you may need to soak them more and keep them really hydrated because that means that they are holding off moisture inside of its body, this is their survival tactic in the wild if they cannot find water in the desert, now since you took on the responsibility of keeping them, it's now your job to make sure that they are well – hydrated and not be stressed out in their environment.

Cost of Keeping Red – Foot Tortoises

Purchase Price

The red – foot tortoise is a relatively affordable pet, hence its wide popularity. If you choose to acquire it from legit reptile breeders, you can expect a price ranging from

Chapter Three: Red - Foot Essentials

$129 to $189 to depending on the breeder as well as the age of the tortoise.

Again, you should consider the availability of space in your home as these tortoises can grow to be quite big as it matures. If you want to buy it for a more affordable price, you may opt to search online if there's any red – foot tortoise in your area being given up for adoption. There are also non-profit and rescue organizations you should visit because rescuing one can be really beneficial to the environment and you can acquire them for a relatively cheaper price or even for free.

Shelter and Accessories

At the onset, it could cost you about $125 or more for its housing needs – that usually includes a 10 – 20 gallon tank or a DIY tortoise table complete with other caging materials for decorations and water bowl. The heaters, UVB lights, basking platforms, hideouts, substrate and other additional fixtures needed could cost more or less $300.

Monthly Food Allowance

Chapter Three: Red - Foot Essentials

You'll probably spend around $40 per week for 30 pounds of vegetables and fruit unless of course you choose to just feed them with grass or weeds found in your backyard. They can live with that but as a keeper, it's probably best to provide them with food that has the right nutrients so that they can grow healthily.

Cage Maintenance

Don't forget to factor in the expense for cage maintenance to remove dirt and bacteria especially in their water bowls. Tortoises pretty much poop a lot that's basically because they are herbivores – they tend to digest and defecate food easily, which means that their tank or enclosure should ideally be cleaned at least every other day to avoid the incidence of parasites, infections and shell rot. You will also want to factor in the yearly electricity costs of keeping a terrarium clean, tempered, lit and conditioned to the needs of the red – foot tortoise.

Breeding Materials

You also need to buy a laying bin if in case you'd be breeding your red – foot tortoises. You can either buy some

Chapter Three: Red - Foot Essentials

kind of reptile container or a standard laying bin in pet stores. The breeding cost will vary depending on the quality, so you should budget about $50 or more for these extra costs.

Vet Checkups

Red – foot tortoises will need minimal medical attention but it is strongly suggested that you take your hatchling pet to the vet after acquiring them to make sure that they are healthy before bringing them home and mixing them with your other tortoise or turtle species.

You'll pretty much need to bring your tortoise to the vet for a quick check up if you choose to breed them as well. But generally speaking, you won't have to worry about huge medical costs or even a pet insurance for these animals – remember, they live very long and healthy lives, there's an even bigger chance of you acquiring an illness than them.

Chapter Three: Red - Foot Essentials

Chapter Four: Health and Wellness

The key to a tortoise's long life is proper diet. The diet of tortoises in general should be high in fiber and calcium yet low in protein and fruit; the kind of food a keeper should feed depends on the type of tortoise. In this case, red – foot tortoises should be fed with hay since it is high in fiber and highly recommended for grassland tortoises like red – foot and other species that originated from humid areas.

Feeding your tortoise is not that hard, in fact, you won't have to worry about it at all. If you happen to have a

Chapter Four: Health and Wellness

backyard outside or some plants, your red – foot can live a happy and healthy life! But since you took on the responsibility of becoming a reputable keeper or breeder, it's probably best that you live up to that by providing them with a healthy nutrition.

Tortoises are worth the investment not only because they're generally low maintenance animals and amazing creatures but also because they can live for a very long time which can give hobbyists many years of pet – owning pleasure. The main ingredient in keeping them both happy and healthy is proper care. Like other household pets, they are not immune to diseases or common health issues, you might experience some problems along the way as they grow older but if you are knowledgeable about these potential health threats you can prevent it from happening or be able to handle it effectively so that your tortoises can maximize their health potential.

In this chapter, you'll learn the nutritional value that your pet needs and some tips on how to serve it to them. This chapter will also delve deeper on the most common illnesses of red - foot tortoises.

Chapter Four: Health and Wellness

Food for Red – Foots

Fresh produce, hay, commercial pellets and occasional fruity treats as well as their natural food in the wild like grass, flowers and weeds can all contribute in the longevity and health of your pet. There are basically two types of hay; timothy hay and alfafa hay.

Alfafa Hay vs. Timothy Hay

Alfafa hay contains high levels of fiber and calcium but it also contain higher levels of protein than timothy hay, so make sure that you don't overfeed your pet red - foot with too much alfafa hay.

Hay can be purchased per bag and are often found in pet shops, groceries and through online retailers. If you don't see hay in the reptile section, you can find stocks in probably the rabbit or guinea pig sections.

Fruits and Veggies

Plants like collard greens, mustard greens and dandelion greens are all nutritious and packed with high

Chapter Four: Health and Wellness

levels of calcium. You can easily purchase collard and mustard greens in grocery stores, dandelion greens on the other hand can be a bit hard to find but you can always have the option to grow your own.

Red - foot tortoises love to eat Dandelion flowers as well as Hibiscus, Rose Petals and Carnation. You can offer them other types of flowers but make sure that they are non - toxic and are not sprayed with fertilizers or pesticides. It could be tempting to buy lots of fresh veggies in supermarkets but you need to keep in mind that these veggies may not be good choices because greens like spinach because it can block the tortoise's ability to absorb calcium.

Some vegetables like peas and green beans contain high levels of protein, Iceberg lettuces should also be avoided because it can cause diarrhea to tortoises since it has high water content. Fruit can be offered as a treat but make sure that you don't overfeed your pet with it or offer fruits that have high water content. Fruits like strawberries, blueberries, raspberry, apple, papaya and mango are good fruits to feed as long as you offer it to them in limited amounts.

Before you offer fresh foods to your red - foot, it's highly recommended that you sprinkled it with a small amount of calcium supplement preferably with Vitamin D3 and without any phosphorous content for each serving.

Other Food Options

Other foods for red - foot tortoises include grass, flowers, and weeds. Keep in mind that in the wild, tortoises graze on the ground which is why grass should also be available. If you don't have plenty of grass around your backyard, you can easily purchase grass seeds so that you can grow your own grass so that your pet red - foot can graze happily outside. If you keep your pet in an outdoor pen, what you can do is plant edible grasses and other plants so that they can have plenty of options.

If you plan to let your pet red - foot graze or if you're picking wild grasses, weeds or other type of vegetation for

Chapter Four: Health and Wellness

them to eat, just make sure to offer them fresh produce that are not sprayed with pesticides.

It's also important to know which plants are toxic so that you don't accidentally give anything poisonous to your tortoise. Toxic plants include aconite, anemone, azalea, begonia, buttercup, bird of paradise, calla lily, cyclamen, daffodil, dianthus, foxglove, hemlock, hydrangea, ivy, lily of the valley, lobelia, mistletoe, nightshade, oleander, prunus, ragwort, rhododendron, and sweet pea among others.

Commercial pellets can also be rotated as part of your pet's diet. You can purchase them through pet stores or online. Just make sure that before you buy one, you check out the list of ingredients contain in each pack. Plan your pet's nutrition accordingly and look forward to spending a long term relationship with your tortoise.

Chapter Four: Health and Wellness

List of Commercial Pellets for Red – Foots

Zoo Med's Tortoise Food Brand

Natural Grassland Food

- Natural Grassland Tortoise Food is a popular prepared food that's also recommended by most tortoise keepers.
- It is formulated for grassland tortoises including red – foot tortoises
- It has no artificial colors, flavors or preservatives
- The pellets are made up of compressed grass
- You can easily soak the pellets with to soften it
- This meal is a hay – based food that can be mixed with veggies to increase the fiber level on your tortoise's meal.
- Contains 26% fiber, 9% crude protein and 2% fat
- Ingredients include the following:
  - suncured oat hay
  - suncured timothy hay
  - soybean hulls
  - wheat middling

Chapter Four: Health and Wellness

- suncured alfalfa meal

Gourmet Tortoise Food

- Gourmet Tortoise Food is a new brand product by Zoo Med
- It has no artificial colors, flavors or preservatives
- It contains pellets, dried carrots, sweet potatoes, flower petals and hibiscus
- Contains 22% fiber, 8% crude protein and 2% fat
- Ingredients include the following:
  - suncured oat hay
  - suncured timothy hay
  - soybean hulls
  - wheat middling
  - suncured alfalfa meal

PMI Nutrition's Mazuri Food Brand

Mazuri Tortoise Diet - Classic Formula

- Mazuri Tortoise Diet is also a highly – recommended tortoise commercial food in the U.S.

Chapter Four: Health and Wellness

- It is ideal for feeding as a supplement particularly for breeding tortoises.
- It can be mixed with dry salad hay to increase fiber content
- It's best for dry land herbivorous tortoises including red – foots
- It has no artificial colors, flavors or preservatives
- The pellets look a bit like dry dog food but a little soft
- It's odorless
- Make sure to soak it for around 10 minutes for a hatchling tortoise.
- Contains 18% fiber, 15% crude protein and 3% fat
- Make sure to remove any wet leftovers after feeding
- Ingredients include the following:
    - Soybean hulls
    - Ground corn
    - Dehulled soybean meal
    - Ground oats
    - Wheat Middlings

Chapter Four: Health and Wellness

Mazuri Tortoise LS Diet – New Formula

- Mazuri started selling a new brand in 2013 which is a newly formulated low – starch food for tortoises
- Contains 22% fiber, around 12% crude protein and around 4% fat
- This product is a little higher in fiber and a bit lower in protein.
- This food is based from timothy hay.
- Ingredients include the following:
    - Timothy hay
    - Ground soybean hulls
    - Dried beet pulp
    - Wheat middlings
    - Oat hulls
- The pellets look a lot like compressed hay mix
- You can soak the dry pellets and mash it. You can also grind it.
- The pellets soften once you soak it and it also doesn't get too mushy
- Contains 22% fiber, around 12% crude protein and around 4% fat

Chapter Four: Health and Wellness

European Mazuri

- The European Mazuri products are lower in fiber and higher in protein.
- PMI Nutrition Int. - Nutrazu (Europe)
- This is the European version of the Mazuri products in the U.S.
- It is designed as a complementary food that's best for dry land herbivorous tortoises.
- It contains 18% fiber, around 15% crude protein and around 3% fat

Dietex Int. - Mazuri Exotic Leaf Eater (U.K.)

- This is not the same reptile food as the Mazuri Tortoise Diet made in the U.S. It's from a different company with different food formula
- It is manufactured in Essex, England
- It contains 11.36% fiber, around 23% protein and around 3% fat
- Other Tortoise Food Pellets
- Agrobs - Pre Alpin Testudo food (Germany)

Chapter Four: Health and Wellness

- This is one of the most popular tortoise food product in Europe
- It contain low protein, low fat but high in fiber
- The low protein unburden the tortoise's liver and kidneys
- Not typically sold in the U.S.
- It is available in various formulations:
  - Pre Alpin Testudo:

    It contains fiber 29.6 %, protein 5.2 %, and fat 2.1 %
  - Pre Alpin Testudo Baby:

    It contains fiber 26.4 %, protein 9.6 %, and fat 2.1 %
  - Pre Alpin Fibre:

    It contains fiber 27.8 %, protein 7.9 %, and fat 2.2 %
  - Pre Alpin Herbs:

    It contains fiber 27.8 %, protein 7.9 %, fat 2.2 %

Ectotherm - Sulcata Gold
  - This food is formulated for grassland tortoises including red – foots
  - The pellets must be soaked for around 30 minutes before feeding it to your pet

Chapter Four: Health and Wellness

- It is now under a new name "Grassland Gold Tortoise Diet"
- It contains 9% fiber, around 7% protein and around 4% fat

Exo Terra - Tortoise Adult Food

- This is suited for adult tortoises and it is also the older version of Exo Terra product by Hagen
- It contains 11% fiber, around 18% protein and around 3% fat

Exo Terra - Soft Pellets European Tortoise Foods

- The Soft Pellets European Tortoise Food is a new brand by Exo Terra. It includes other food meals such as Soft Pellets Adult European Tortoise Food and Soft Pellets Juvenile European Tortoise Food.
- This food product is best for European grassland tortoises including red – foots, Hermann's, and Russian tortoises.
- The pellets can be moistened to make it quite soft
- It's packed in a dark jar to preserve its nutrients

Chapter Four: Health and Wellness

- It contains the following percentages:
  - Soft Pellets Adult European Tortoise Food:

  It contains fiber 26 %, protein 9 %, and fat 2 %
  - Soft Pellets Juvenile European Tortoise Food:

  It contains fiber 24 %, protein 11 %, and fat 2 %

Fluker - Tortoise Diet

- This food contains land turtle formula
- It contains 13% fiber, around 8% protein and around 3% fat

Happy Pet Products Ltd - Komodo Complete Holistic Tortoise Diet

- This is formulated for European reptile species
- It's another popular tortoise food in Europe
- It's available in many flavors
- Quite hard to find in the U.S
- It contains 12% fiber, around 9% protein and around 5% fat

Chapter Four: Health and Wellness

Marion Zoological - Mozaic Reptile Food (Tortoise)

- This food is intended as a primary diet for reptiles such as tortoises and also iguanas. It can be a supplementary diet for turtles.
- It contains 11% fiber, around 20% protein and around 6% fat

Pretty Bird International - Pretty Pets Tortoise Food

- It is available in small and large tortoise versions
- It contains 13% fiber, around 8% protein and around 3% fat

Rep - Cal - Tortoise Food

- This is by Rep – Cal Research Labs
- It contains 18% fiber, around 16% protein and around 1% fat

Repashy - Grassland Grazer

- The Grassland Grazer is a new product by Repashy
- It has a gel formula that's well – suited for species that are mostly herbivores including tortoises.

Chapter Four: Health and Wellness

- It contains 30% crude fiber, 15% crude protein and 3% crude fat

T-Rex - Tortoise Dry Formula

- It contains 10% fiber, 13% protein and 3% fat

Zeigler - Tortoise Monster Diet

- This is formulated for land tortoises including Sulcata, Red – foots, Yellow - foots, Leopard, Russian, Gopher, and Pancake tortoises
- It contains 8% fiber, 12% crude protein and 5% crude fat

Don't Overfeed Them!

Both in the wild and captivity, red – footed tortoises are omnivores. This means that they eat various types of food compared to other tortoise species. However, even if they are not finicky eaters, you don't want to overfeed them especially foods that are rich with animal protein. They can only consume a small serving of moistened low – fat food. They may also eat lean meat but make sure that it's only one ounce

Chapter Four: Health and Wellness

– this is particularly for adult red – foot tortoises. You can offer these every other week if you feel the need to offer it. Don't overdose them with animal protein, so to speak as it won't be good for their health.

Their diet should also include various fresh and leafy veggies including mustard greens, dandelion greens, escarole, and endive. However, you need to also monitor the calcium to phosphorous rations that are found in veggies. Other food you can offer includes fruits, vitamin D3 and calcium supplement. We will delve deeper on the nutrition section of the book.

Improper Diet May Lead to Health Issues

Improper diet and lack of calcium are some of the culprits of shell rotting among tortoises and turtles alike. The lack or absence of UVB lighting can cause the shell to slowly degenerate, deteriorate and soften. This can also be cause by lack of calcium which in the long run will weaken its structure and make its bones soft, eventually leading up to the shell.

Chapter Four: Health and Wellness

If your red – foot tortoises displays signs of soft spots, fluid beneath the surface of its plates, oozing pus or discharge, foul smell, shell plates falling off and exposing skin tissue, then that's a clear sign that the shell has rot. You will need to investigate its habitat for the root cause of the fungal or bacterial infection. Too much moisture or too little of it, improper diet, improper heating or lighting and unsanitary conditions are either one or all to blame for shell rot.

A tortoise's shell could also have been scratched, punctured or damaged by a sharp object in the enclosure so ensure that you remove any sharp edged objects and that the whole cage has been cleaned, sanitized, has safe materials, and is kept at the required temperature fit for grassland tortoises needs.

Parasites and worms find their way into a tortoise's enclosure/tank in a number of ways. To prevent your pet's enclosure in being infested with parasites or other harmful insects, you will want to clean out the enclosure and all its fixtures to make sure there is no leftover food or hidden poops that could become a breeding ground for

Chapter Four: Health and Wellness

parasites. Scrub down the enclosure and dry out all the cage fixtures before placing them back. Make sure that you have scrubbed all the corners of the enclosure and rinse them off thoroughly.

Make sure to bring your red - foot tortoise to the vet for a quick visit or routine check up to make sure that it is not infested with worms and if this should be the case, to give it the proper treatment it needs before returning it to its enclosure. Thorough cleaning and routine checkup provides a bit of guarantee that parasites won't worsen or spread out to your other collection in the future.

Proper Lighting Requirements

When it comes to housing these tortoises, since they are native in tropical areas it means that they naturally prefer a humid environment. You need to provide an enclosure complete with a secure lid so that you can place them outdoors when they get bigger. Make sure to use a mister in order to increase the tank's humidity if need be.

Chapter Four: Health and Wellness

Ideally, you want your pet to have a space that's densely planted with vegetation because that's where they will sometimes retreat and relax. You can also use a doghouse – type shelter for adult red – foots. Make sure to heat their enclosure if temperatures drop below 65 to 70 degrees Fahrenheit at night. During the day, they can still do well if temperatures reach up to 95 degrees.

The walls of your pet's enclosure should ideally measure 16 in high, and it should go a few inches deep in order to prevent your pet from digging their way out of it and escaping.

If you choose to house your pet inside, make sure to buy a large enclosure (ideally 4 ft. x 6 ft.), you need to also provide a cypress bark as a substrate in order to maintain humidity levels. We will focus more on these on the next few chapters.

Reptiles need lighting which is why your pet red – foot would need a UVA/ UVB light especially if you're going to place them on an indoor enclosure. The cage should be heated using heat bulbs. Make sure to provide a basking spot that measures around 95 degrees. It shouldn't go lower than 80 degrees Fahrenheit.

If the enclosure drops below 70 degrees especially at night, your pet red – foot can develop hypothermia or a respiratory illness. Make sure to provide them with a pan of water, so that your pet can easily access it plus it will also kept the cage humid. You also need to provide a hide at the cooler side of the tank because this will allow your pet to retreat.

During colder months, you can expect your pet to slow down but red – foot tortoises don't hibernate like other reptiles.

Health Issues Related to Improper Lighting

Lung infections are very common among tortoises like the red - foot especially if the species came from the wild and were sold illegally from other countries. The shipping of pets from their native land to other countries can put these tortoises under a lot of stress. Factor in the unsanitary living

Chapter Four: Health and Wellness

conditions and poor husbandry practices from breeders just trying to make a quick buck off of these pets.

If your pet tortoises are crowdedly packed and shipped in a tight spaced box or enclosure with no food or water during their travel time. Once they arrived, often times, these tortoises and even turtle species already became lethargic, lost some weight and have suffered from respiratory infections. Of course, if your pet red - foot is kept in captivity and you've bought them from legitimate hobbyists and these breeders raised them in captivity as well, there is lesser chance of them being diagnosed with lung problems. Nevertheless, it is still seen even among captive breeds.

Respiratory diseases can be detected through a physical exam by a reptile vet. You'll also have a clue if your pet will be pre – disposed to this type of illness if you've found out where they came from or how they are raised.

Chapter Four: Health and Wellness

Usually radiographs and blood samples are used to diagnose such disease, and the treatment is antibiotics. The disease can lasts for several weeks and even months depending on how severe the condition is before being treated. Antibiotics and nasal drops can be orally given but most tortoises especially the ill ones often withdraw and hide in their shell which is why the treatment is just injected for easier and faster application.

Most vets will show you how to administer the injection; it's quite easy once you've learned how to do it. These antibiotics will enable your tortoise to clearly smell and tastes its food better. If the tortoise is already severely ill because of respiratory infections, a feeding tube will be placed and the tortoise will need to undergo surgery to attach the tube on its neck just so the tortoise can eat and recover. It can take several weeks to months until the animal can eat on its own.

Owners can aid their pets during the process by keeping their tortoises warm. Vets will suggest keepers that

Chapter Four: Health and Wellness

the tortoises should be kept indoor during treatment and provide them with heat or a full lighting.

Chapter Five: Handling and Grooming Red – Foot Tortoises

Red – foot tortoises are solitary animals and they are very unlikely to bite someone unless of course if they are provoked, threatened or mishandled. A red – foot tortoise or hatchlings can be safely held by the sides of its shell just like how you would hold other tortoise species. Handling baby red – foot tortoise is quite easy but this could also cause them to be stressed if they are not being handled properly. Improper and sometimes inappropriate handling will make these creatures feel unsafe and uncomfortable, and it could

Chapter Five: Handling & Grooming Red – Foot Tortoises

cause potential aggression as well. Handling your tortoise while they are still hatchlings or juveniles is a great training for them because it teaches them how to socialize and become tamed when being touched. Although, tortoises and turtles in general are non – threatening animals, they can still become aggressive if they aren't tamed properly. One of the best ways in taming them is through proper handling.

You can have your red - foot tortoise get used to you by just carrying them around while they're still young, just keep them around the house or with other same species so that your pet can be socialized. If your pet is socialized, it can make them less shy when being touched or viewed. Some hatchlings will be quite skittish at first which is why you need to also be careful in handling them so that they won't get traumatize by the experience otherwise they could hate being around with people or be wary to being touched. In this chapter, you'll learn how to handle your pet red - foot and also give you instructions on how to groom them so that you can maintain their gorgeous shells and health.

Chapter Five: Handling & Grooming Red – Foot Tortoises

How to Handle a Red – Foot Tortoise

Picking up a tortoise is fairly easy when they're young, you just simply have to grab the bottom and top art of their shell just right in the center using your fingers so that they won't be able to push you off or slide off. Once your tortoise is calm and assuming that they're properly socialized, you can let them walk around your palms but don't raise them up too high as they could slip out and fall especially when they get older and stronger. Properly hold their shells and apply a tight grip on the center top and bottom. Never hold the side of the shells because their rear legs can easily push your finger and they could fall off.

When your tortoise gets a bit larger and heavier, you should start holding both sides of the top and bottom shell using your hands to provide support. Sometimes juvenile tortoises will push you off using their feet, so you just need to have a slightly tight grip over them but of course, not to the point of squeezing them too hard. Make sure to wash your hands after holding your tortoises because they can

Chapter Five: Handling & Grooming Red – Foot Tortoises

potentially have salmonella. It's also a good practice to wash your hands before holding them, and try not to touch their face, eyes, mouths or legs too much.

Once your pet red - foot reaches maturity and has become full grown, you obviously won't be able to simply hold them even with your hands; it will totally require some heavy lifting on your part. Just make sure to handle them carefully, try not to put them on their backs and support the shell with both hands. If you think you can't lift them up because they're too heavy, it's probably best to let someone help you so that you won't risk dropping your tortoise and possibly damaging their shell.

Wash Your Hands After Handling Them

Reptiles and amphibians such as red – foot tortoises are usually carriers of the Salmonella bacteria which is why we highly recommend that you quarantine your pet. All new tortoises should be isolated from the rest of your other animals especially turtle collection for around 2 to 3 months. In this time period you can assess the health status of your pet as well as its behavior. You can also opt to bring your pet

Chapter Five: Handling & Grooming Red – Foot Tortoises

to the veterinarian during the quarantine stage for fecal evaluation and wellness exam. Quarantine also requires that the dish, food, accessories and cleaning of the red – foot tortoise is done separately from other materials you use if you have any other pets.

Salmonella bacteria can cause salmonellosis to humans. It is classified as a gastro – intestinal disorder that can lead to diarrhea, vomiting, fever and also abdominal cramps. In worst case scenarios, salmonella can also spread to the human brain, bones and blood.

You can't tell if your pet is a carrier of the salmonella bacteria which is why in 1975, after the salmonella outbreak in the United States, the Food and Drug Administration started regulating the sale of turtle species with a top shell length of around 4 inches long. The best way to protect you, your family and also your other pet collection from the possibility of getting infected by the Salmonella bacteria is to simply wash your hands thoroughly before and after you handle your tortoise. Make sure to do it immediately right after handling them and remind yourself not to touch your mouth before washing your hands.

Chapter Five: Handling & Grooming Red – Foot Tortoises

During the quarantine period, young children should be kept away because they are at greater risk of developing various complications due to the spread of Salmonella bacteria, and it's hard for their body to combat the disease since their immune system is not fully mature yet. Children are also more likely to put their hands in their mouths after touching a turtle which can quickly transfer the bacteria to their bodies.

The Center for Disease Control and Prevention recommends that those living with children less than five years old should not even keep any type of amphibian or reptile. This is in addition to the much greater risk of a child being bitten by your red – foot tortoise. If you already own one, and you have young children at home, make sure to supervise them when interacting with these pets, wash their hands thoroughly, and as much as possible don't let them get near these creatures until they are quite old enough.

Provide a Clean Environment

Dirty water could potentially kill your pet or make him more susceptible to various health issues. You need to be vigilant against all the threats that could potentially harm

Chapter Five: Handling & Grooming Red – Foot Tortoises

your red – foot tortoise. If you want to seek professional help, you can always ask your veterinarian for more tips on how to clean its indoor tank. You can feed your pet outside in a separate tank. Create a separate tank for feeding, this might be an additional task, but you can be assured that there will be no uneaten food floating around the water region.

Many people are confused when someone tells them to groom their tortoises, for the most part, it looks like they don't really need a bath since they don't shed, they are used to being dirty since they're constantly walking in the ground, grazing the grass and they can still be considered wild animals – and wild animals don't take a bath.

There's another tortoise misconception out there that if you bought a particular commercial product for your pet's shell it could make it shiny and or could give the shell some sort of nutrients. That's not true and most of the time these products are harmful since they have chemical content.

The carapace (top shell) and plastron (bottom shell) of your tortoise is composed of tissues, pores, keratin, and nerves, it requires sunlight and oxygen to keep them healthy

Chapter Five: Handling & Grooming Red – Foot Tortoises

so if you apply wax, oils or other commercial products it can accumulate and clog your tortoise's pores which can eventually lead to problems. So if you want to keep your tortoise's shell "shiny" and keep them clean, all they need is a clean water, container, and good old tooth brush. Of course, you may need to adjust the brush as they get bigger.

Young or juvenile red - foot tortoises are quite easy to clean because you can still handle them, but once they reach their full size, you may need to rethink how you're going to clean them up or decide on how you're going to house them. Usually you just need to provide a small water lagoon in your yard or garden where your tortoise can easily access and soak in thereby naturally cleaning themselves up.

Grooming a tortoise is not a necessity because they're simply used to getting dirty, but again, since you took on the responsibility of keeping one, it's your job to make sure that they are clean and receive occasionally bathing for health's sake and to also prevent spreading of dirt around the house or its enclosure – the best part is, it's completely safe to do so. To start off, you need a container, water, toothbrush, cotton buds, towel/ dry cloth. Place your tortoise in the tub

Chapter Five: Handling & Grooming Red – Foot Tortoises

and allow it to hydrate himself for about 10 minutes to 20 minutes, after which you can replace the water. Fill the container again with clean water that is no deeper than the tortoise's plastron and just about a few centimeters deep above its top shell.

Once you do, you should again allow your pet to rehydrate and replace their water stores. While your tortoise is doing that, you can now prepare your bathing tools like a toothbrush. Keep in mind that you don't need to put any kind of soap, detergent, oils, shampoo or other cleaning materials that has chemical content. Just a fresh clean water and toothbrush will do.

Your main objective here is to just simply clean out the shell and their legs, they're not supposed to smell good or even look good like other household pets. Once you've prepared your brush, just gently brush their top shell particularly the areas where dirt can often build up as well as the sides. Make sure to clean their scutes and you can also slightly clean their head, legs, neck and tail using cotton buds. When brushing their body parts that are not covered with scales or shells, make sure to gently rub it because these areas could be sensitive. Clean up their claws thoroughly since this is one of the dirtiest parts of your tortoise's body.

After cleaning the top and side of the shells, you can gently flip them over to clean the bottom shell or the plastron. Pay attention to the dirt between their scutes and rub it carefully. Once you're done removing the dirt, you can now rinse them with water. Don't use any unnecessary product (unless recommended by your vet) because it can be fatal for some tortoise. These products can mix with water and your tortoise can ingest it.

Tortoises don't really shed skin but sometimes you can see their paper thin scutes peeling off like fragments, it's quite normal and you can aid in removing that whenever you are brushing them up because it can allow for a much healthier shell. After you have rinsed them off, take them out of the water, and dry them up using a soft towel or cloth. Gently do this at least once or twice a week or even once a month (it's entirely up to you) so that your tortoise can be nice and clean.

Chapter Five: Handling & Grooming Red – Foot Tortoises

If you are properly following the husbandry tips and feeding your pet with a healthy diet, their shell will naturally shine by itself without the need for any product. The main advantage of bathing your tortoise is that, it gives an opportunity for owners to thoroughly examine or check their pet if there'll be any sign of illness, shell rot, injury or even abrasion. Occasional cleaning will make your tortoise feel neat, happy and healthy. This procedure will also maintain their skin and avoid the rotting of their shells.

Chapter Five: Handling & Grooming Red – Foot Tortoises

Chapter Six: Breeding Season for Red – Foot Tortoises

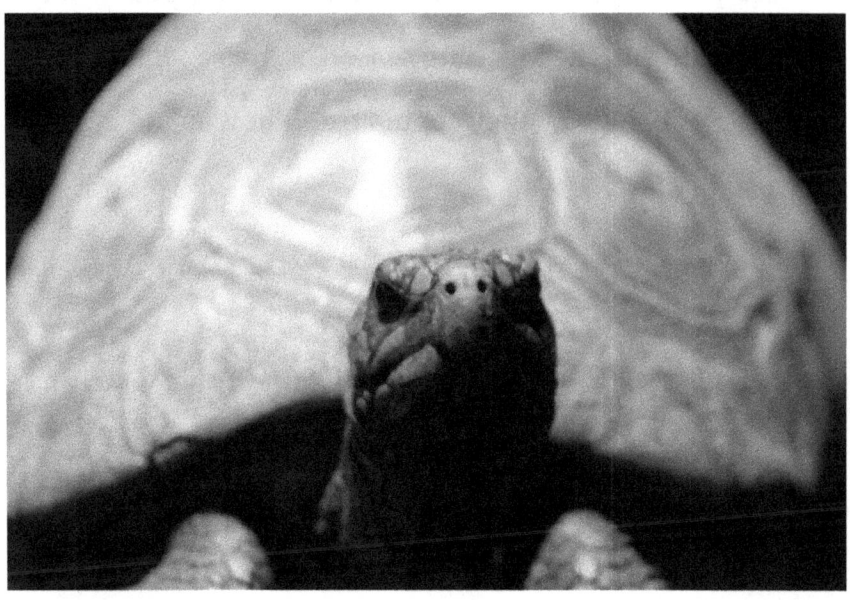

Red - foot tortoises can usually mate the entire year but their breeding season happens during autumn when the temperature in the morning is a bit cooler. In the wild and even in captivity, males court females by directly chasing them and getting in front of them. They will not stop until a female tortoise completely stops so that the male can mount her and start mating. When they these animals copulate, you can expect grunts and loud noises.

If you house a female with a male tortoise and the space is not large enough, males can sometimes damage the

Chapter Six: Breeding Season for Red – Foot Tortoises

female by aggressively chasing her or like what was mentioned in the previous chapter, the female can get stressed out. You may want to always check flipped tortoises especially during the breeding season. In this chapter you'll learn more about how they copulate and how many eggs they usually lay.

Male or Female?

Red - foot tortoises are sexually dimorphic which means that you can easily identify which one is male or female based on their physical characteristics. Although both sexes look identical, males have concave bottom shells with thicker and longer tales. Their rectal openings are also quite wide than females. They are also larger and have a more prominent gular On the other hand, females are relatively smaller than male red – foots and their anal scutes in their plastron has a much smaller opening than that of the males.

Mating Season

Nesting usually happens around 6 to 8 weeks after copulation, you'll know this when you see your female red –

Chapter Six: Breeding Season for Red – Foot Tortoises

foots digging holes using its front legs. They usually burrow against a wall or near a tree/plant. Once they complete their digging process, the female excavates their egg chamber and starts laying eggs. They usually cover their nest in a meticulous way and the whole nesting process can take hours. Just like most tortoises, red – foots take a long time to cover their nest, sometimes it could take them two to three days just to make sure that the eggs are fully covered. During this time, some female red – foots can also become overly aggressive if they found out that people or other species are near their nests.

Be careful if you're going to aid in their nesting process because some tortoises can attempt to bite you and will try to push you away using their shells just to protect their nests. Red – foots tortoises can produce many eggs in a year; the average clutch size is 5 during the breeding season with about 12 to 25 eggs or more. These species really lay lots of eggs which is why red – foots are abundant in the U.S.

Chapter Six: Breeding Season for Red – Foot Tortoises

Once you see that your female had laid eggs, make sure that they're not looking or is far from you when you dig up their eggs. You have to get the eggs and place it in a container for proper incubation and to protect it against potential predation. Incubate the eggs at around 80 to 85 degrees and moistened them with a bit of water. The eggs will usually hatch after 100 to 120 days. Once the hatchlings comes out of the shells, just leave them be in their container until their yolks are fully absorbed, after which you can put the young hatchlings in soft towels until you see their bottom shell is sealed.

Breed Like a Hobbyists

When it comes to breeding and raising red – foot tortoises, it is best that you seek help from a hobbyist. You may also consider acquiring one from a hobbyist either directly or through pet conventions so that you can have more options.

The great thing about hobbyists is that you can ask them questions about how they raise these tortoises, the

Chapter Six: Breeding Season for Red – Foot Tortoises

requirements and specifications they would need as well as why they're doing it. You can easily see why it's better to buy one from them than from a pet store because these breeders are passionate about their pets and very knowledgeable about them. After all they're the ones who raised them.

However, you should also look out for private breeders that are just looking to make cash out of these creatures because they could be breeding for its sake. You don't want to get a tortoise that are pre – matured or somewhat sick looking due to bad breeding practices or poor husbandry.

Be wary of such breeders, who are claiming to be hobbyists, because there are a lot of them out there. They could have smuggled pets from foreign sources or must have picked them out from the wild which is illegal based on several wildlife organizations. When it comes to purchasing pet tortoises, always buy it from a breeder that is reputable, trustworthy, and passionate and also a professional. In the next section, you'll learn the qualities to

Chapter Six: Breeding Season for Red – Foot Tortoises

look out for on a breeder and the characteristics of a healthy red - foot tortoise.

Chapter Seven: Maintenance Tips for Red – Foot Tortoises

This chapter will delve deeper on how to house and take care of adult red - foot tortoises. Once they become fully mature, obviously you won't be able to contain them in their previous enclosures. If you don't have a big backyard or you only have a limited space, you can still house them comfortably by creating a play pen where they can be free to roam around outside your house yet preventing them from getting away. You'll learn how to build a pen and the ideal location of your growing tortoises. You'll also get some tips

Chapter Seven: Maintenance Tips for Red – Foot Tortoises

on how to protect them against predators so that they will be safe walking outside.

Building a Tortoise Pen

As you now know, red - foot tortoises are better off living outside since these creatures are originally land dwellers or grassland species. Once they become huge, the best habitat for them is outdoors so that they can also get direct heat from the sun to make them healthy. Artificial UVB bulbs or lights may not be sufficient for them anymore, ultraviolet rays from the sun is now a necessity because it will aid in the production of Vitamin D3 which will help your tortoise absorb the calcium that they need to keep their body and shell healthy.

If your red - foot tortoise becomes too large for your house inside, it's time to relocate them by creating a tortoise or turtle pen. The bigger the pen, the better for your tortoise, this is because it will replicate their habitat in the wild which is much ideal for them.

Chapter Seven: Maintenance Tips for Red – Foot Tortoises

When building a play pen, you also have to make sure that they are not overcrowded; this is for owners who are considering of keeping more than one red - foot tortoise or housing them with other tortoise or turtle species. Overcrowding can lead to poor hygiene and even territoriality issues among inhabitants. The ideal pen size for tortoises in general should be 3 sq. ft. per each inch of its shell. Juvenile or growing red - foots can be housed in a pen that's about 4 x 3 feet in size; adult tortoises should be double or triple than the recommended size.

Play Pen for Your Red - foot

Building a play pen for your adult red - foot tortoises is just like designing their enclosure when they were still young and small. You can basically get creative and just let your imagination and taste for aesthetic run wild. There are no specific rules but the guidelines below can give you an idea on how to build one or where to place one if you have a larger space outside.

- Step #1: Build your pen in a space where your tortoise can have lots of sunshine

Chapter Seven: Maintenance Tips for Red – Foot Tortoises

- Step #2: You can also choose to place it in a sort of slope or elevated soil if you have one so that your tortoise can easily turn itself back up if it gets flipped over.

- Step #3: Place it in a spot where it is safe from any hazard or drainage since it can be prone to flooding

If you are located in a place where the climate has hot summers and relatively cold winters, you can possibly let them stay outdoors all year round because that could be an ideal temperature for your pet red - foot. If that's not the case and the condition may be too harsh for your pet especially at night, you can still let them play outside every morning or at least throughout the day to catch some sunlight and also get some exercise.

If you have enough space outside, you can try building a green house where your tortoise can bask in and stay heated if the temperature outside are too cold for them. You can choose to build something that has a plastic roof on

Chapter Seven: Maintenance Tips for Red – Foot Tortoises

top so that the sun's infrared rays can still pass through and still benefit your tortoise.

The basking spot should be around 90 degrees Fahrenheit or a bit higher than that since these creatures prefer warmer temperature just like in the desert. If you built a green house, the sun can still heat up the enclosure at about 18 degrees Fahrenheit warmer than the cooler temperature outside the green house.

Tortoise Ratio

Aside from the recommended size of the pen or green house enclosure that you will build outside for your adult tortoise, you also need to think about the ratio of the male and female tortoise if you're going to house them in the same enclosure. If you don't want them to breed or if you only have a limited space outside, you should just stick to keeping female tortoises. This is because female tortoises get along better than their counterparts. If you own a couple of male tortoises, you should also make sure to separate them or as much as possible not housed them in one enclosure as they tend to become aggressive towards other male tortoises.

Chapter Seven: Maintenance Tips for Red – Foot Tortoises

If you house both male and female tortoises together, make sure that the ratio is 1:4 (one male to 4 females); this is because male tortoises are known to chasing female tortoises constantly, if the female tortoise is always getting chased, she can get stressed out and this could lead to her getting sick. As much as possible, don't house different tortoises or turtles in one enclosure unless you have a really huge backyard where they can have more than enough space to be separated from one another.

Secure Your Pet Red - foot

The main disadvantage of letting your pet roam around outside is that you won't be able to always supervise them, and while you can eliminate the risks of hazards by placing the pen or green house in a safe location, they could still be at risk because of predators – this will include your other household pets like cats or dogs, smaller pests like ants and real outside predators like raccoons, birds or other wild animals.

Chapter Seven: Maintenance Tips for Red – Foot Tortoises

One of the biggest threats to tortoises are dogs, there have been many cases where a dog is housetrained and properly socialize to get along with other pets but because of animal instinct for some reason, owners often end up finding that their dog has caused serious injury to their pet tortoises or turtles. Make sure to supervise your dog if you're going to let him mingle with your tortoise and never leave your pet red - foot on its own devises. This is why your tortoise pen should preferably have a fence or a border as well as a rooftop of some sort for added protection against other animals.

Another common threat for tortoises living outside is pests and insects like fire ants, bees and other poisonous creatures. Your tortoise will surely munch on the grass or plants nearby but the problem is that this is also where such harmful insects hang out or lives to prevent this from happening; you can use a bait trap so that these ants will die or use other alternatives. Don't spray pesticides because your tortoise can absorb these chemicals and cause them to get sick.

Chapter Seven: Maintenance Tips for Red – Foot Tortoises

Index

abilities 1, 10
adult 5, 6, 9, 11, 13, 16, 20, 28, 29, 42, 45, 55, 59, 60, 61, 64, 77, 99, 100
adults 9, 19, 28, 31, 32, 100
age 26, 40, 41
aggressive 3, 4, 7, 12, 13, 14, 20, 23, 56, 57, 105
amphibians 24, 48, 99, 104
aquatic 3, 10, 16, 42, 57, 59, 61, 68, 75, 79
Aquatic – Lives in water. 96
Arboreal – Lives in trees. 96
bask 8, 15, 18, 79
bottom 15, 16, 18, 19, 28, 47, 67, 80, 82, 88, 97, 100
breeding season 2, 24
captive – bred 3, 15
captivity 2, 15, 24, 40, 50, 58, 63, 85, 99, 100, 105
claws 16, 27, 46
cloaca 6, 24
Clutch – A batch of eggs. 97
common snapping turtle 5, 6, 7, 20
conditions 12, 56, 65, 66, 76, 95, 99
eating. 97
Convention on International Trade in Endangered Species of Wild Fauna and Flora 30
copulation 56, 59, 62
creatures 10, 14, 23, 46, 50, 63
dealers 25, 27
debris 70, 72, 73, 81, 87
degrees 15, 19, 65, 67
diet 11, 12, 37, 38, 39, 40, 60, 71, 72, 73, 76, 99
disease 27, 34, 49, 68, 71, 101
dominant 57
eat 10, 23, 37, 39, 40, 41, 43, 60, 72, 82, 85
eggs 2, 8, 9, 26, 29, 30, 58, 59, 62, 70, 97, 99, 100
enclosures 16, 18, 33
environment 26, 31, 33, 35, 42, 43, 46, 58, 83, 95, 97
features 4, 22, 79
feeding 37, 39, 41, 42, 43, 52, 56, 67
female 2, 24, 29, 55, 56, 57, 58, 59, 61, 62, 97, 98, 99, 100

fertilization	58
filter	17, 50, 52, 73, 76, 81, 88
fishes	10, 23, 39, 40, 51
food	7, 4, 31, 37, 38, 39, 42, 43, 48, 52, 60, 71, 72, 96
Food and Drug Administration	49
Freshwater	10
fruits	39, 40, 72
gallons	17, 81, 89
habitats	7
hatchlings	9, 10, 15, 19, 26, 27, 29, 32, 35, 37, 46, 56, 60, 61, 100
health	4, 7, 3, 10, 26, 36, 38, 41, 44, 48, 51, 66, 69, 106
healthy	12, 23, 25, 32, 33, 36, 38, 40, 55, 65, 66, 82, 85
hibernate	65, 66
hide	10, 76, 78, 79, 88, 99
hiding spot	19
humidifier	35
hunters	10
husbandry	13, 70
illnesses	60, 68, 70, 72
infection	68, 72, 73, 79
juvenile	4, 10, 13, 20, 28, 41, 45, 62, 78, 85
keeper	4, 13, 19, 20, 46
lamp	34, 84
length	16, 27, 30, 40, 49, 54, 75, 76, 77, 84
light	33, 34, 35, 36, 60, 85
longevity	1
Male	6, 24, 56, 59
Mates	61
Mating	61
mature	24, 27, 49, 55, 61
nesting spot	2
owners	2, 28, 51, 53, 63, 85, 88
oxygen	50, 66, 67, 82, 89
Pet stores	51
plastron	7, 19, 20
ponds	7, 14, 18, 24, 79
populations	9, 10, 29
predation	9, 60
predators	9, 10, 47, 80
private breeders	2
pump	19, 67, 81, 83, 86, 87, 89

pumps 17, 76, 86, 87, 88
Quarantine.. 48
reptiles 24, 32, 51, 98, 99, 104
requirements 15, 31, 41
Salmonella bacteria 48, 49, 86
season..7, 35, 41, 55, 57, 80
sex... 24, 58, 100
sexual maturity 61
shallow.. 3, 16, 33, 35, 60, 78, 79, 81, 105
size 6, 7, 12, 14, 17, 24, 28, 39, 40, 50, 52, 75, 76, 77, 78
Snapping Turtle............................ 1, 12, 14, 22, 23, 38, 61, 65, 66, 68, 75, 76, 77, 104, 105
species 3, 1, 2,
   3, 4, 5, 7, 8, 9, 10, 12, 13, 15, 20, 25, 26, 27, 34, 46, 49, 59, 64, 66, 68, 69, 79, 98, 105
subspecies 3, 6
substrate... 35, 52, 73, 78
supplies.. 32
tank.................... 15, 16, 17, 33, 35, 50, 51, 52, 53, 70, 72, 76, 77, 78, 85, 86, 87, 88, 96
temperature...12, 15, 19,
   31, 32, 34, 36, 58, 59, 65, 67, 69, 70, 73, 76, 80, 84, 85, 96, 98, 100
territories.. 3, 61
The Center for Biological Diversity 30
top shell 2, 6, 7, 19, 20, 49, 84
tub 17, 86
turtles 3, 1, 2, 3, 4, 5, 6, 7, 8, 9, 10, 11, 12, 13, 14, 15, 16, 17, 18, 19, 20, 23, 24, 25, 26,
   27, 28, 29, 30, 31, 32, 33, 34, 35, 37, 39, 40, 41, 42, 46, 47, 48, 50, 55, 56, 57, 58, 61,
   63, 64, 65, 66, 68, 69, 70, 75, 76, 77, 79, 81, 82, 83, 84, 85, 96, 103, 104, 105
vet..6, 53, 64, 68, 69, 74
weather 31, 80
wild 2, 15, 24, 29, 37, 39, 50, 57, 62, 65, 66, 85, 104

Glossary

Acclimation – Adjusting to a new environment or new conditions over a period of time

Acrylic Aquarium – Glass aquarium alternative, usually lighter than an ordinary aquarium but can be easily scratched.

Active range – The area of activity which can include hunting, seeking refuge, and finding a mate

Ambient temperature – The overall temperature of the environment

Amelanistic – Amel for short; without melanin, or without any black or brown coloration.

Ammonia – made up of nitrogen and hydrogen. It has an unpleasant smell that's also toxic and corrosive. Leftover food in the enclosure can be contributing factors that build up ammonia

Anerythristic – Anery for short; without any red coloration.

Aquatic – Lives in water.

Arboreal – Lives in trees.

Bacteria – microorganisms that are distributed widely in the environments. Turtle keepers should be aware of the harmful effects of bacteria

Bacteria Bloom – sometimes referred to as a tank syndrome.

Basking – a procedure where tortoises or turtles warms or dries up their body. Tortoises/turtles will need to have a basking area at a certain temperature to prevent shell rot. It also allows absorption of UVA and UVB for thermoregulation

Betadine – An antiseptic that can be used to clean wounds in reptiles

Bilateral – Where stripes, spots or markings are present on both sides of an animal.

Biotic – The living components of an environment.

Bridge – part of the shell that's located in the middle of the front and black legs connecting the top and bottom shell.

Brumation – The equivalent of mammalian hibernation among reptiles

Cannibalistic – Where an animal feeds on others of its own kind.

Cloaca – also vent; a half-moon shaped opening for digestive waste disposal and sexual organs.

Cloacal Gaping – Indication of sexual receptivity of the female.

Cloacal Gland – A gland at the base of the tail which emits foul smelling liquid as a defense mechanism; also called Anal Gland.

Clutch – A batch of eggs.

Constriction – The act of wrapping or coiling around a prey to subdue and kill it prior to eating.

Crepuscular – Active at twilight, usually from dusk to dawn.

Diurnal – Active by day

Drop – To lay eggs or to bear live young

Ectothermic – Cold-blooded. An animal that cannot regulate its own body temperature, but sources body heat from the surroundings

Endemic – Indigenous to a specific region or area.

Estivation – Also Aestivation; a period of dormancy that usually occurs during the hot or dry seasons in order to escape the heat or to remain hydrated.

Flexarium – A reptile enclosure that is mostly made from mesh screening, for species that require plenty of ventilation.

Fossorial – A burrowing species.

Gestation – The period of development of an embryo within a female.

Gravid – The equivalent of pregnant in reptiles

Gut-loading – Feeding insects within 24 hours to a prey before they are fed to your pet, so that they pass on the nutritional benefits

Hatchling – A newly hatched, or baby, reptile.

Herps/Herpetiles – A collective name for reptile and amphibian species.

Herpetoculturist – A person who keeps and breeds reptiles in captivity

Herpetologist – A person who studies ectothermic animals, sometimes also used for those who keeps reptiles.

Herpetology – The study of reptiles and amphibians.

Hide Box – A furnishing within a reptile cage that gives the animal a secure place to hide.

Husbandry – The daily care of a pet reptile.

Hygrometer – Used to measure humidity.

Impaction – A blockage in the digestive tract due to the swallowing of an object that cannot be digested or broken down.

Incubate – Maintaining eggs in conditions favorable for development and hatching.

Juvenile – Not yet adult; not of breedable age

LTC – Long Term Captive; or one that has been in captivity for more than six months.

MBD – Metabolic Bone Disease; occurs when reptiles lack sufficient calcium in their diet.

Morph – Color pattern

Musking – Secretion of a foul smelling liquid from its vent as a defense mechanism.

Oviparous – Egg-bearing.

Ovoviviparous – Eggs are retained inside the female's body until they hatch.

Popping – The process by which the sex is determined among hatchlings.

Probing – The process by which the sex is determined among adults.

Sloughing – Shedding.

Sub-adult – Juvenile

Substrate – The material lining the bottom of a reptile enclosure.

Stat – Short for Thermostat

Tag – Slang for a bite or being bitten

Terrarium – A reptile enclosure.

Thermo-regulation – The process by which cold-blooded animals regulate their body temperature by moving from hot to cold surroundings.

Vent – Cloaca

Vivarium – Glass-fronted enclosure

Viviparous – Gives birth to live young.

WC – Wild Caught

WF – Wild Farmed; refers to the collection of a pregnant female whose eggs or young were hatched or born in captivity.

Yearling – A year old.

Zoonosis – A disease that can be passed from animal to man

Photo Credits

Page 1 Photo by user Kurt Bauschardt via Flickr.com

https://www.flickr.com/photos/kurt-b/4748200556/

Page 4 Photo by user Carlos Bustamante via Flickr.com

https://www.flickr.com/photos/fuchales/8224044942/

Page 22 Photo by user David Schenfeld via Flickr.com

https://www.flickr.com/photos/schenfeld/6219227990/

Page 35 Photo by user Paul Ritchie via Flickr.com

https://www.flickr.com/photos/thelizardwizard/3729324802/

Page 50 Photo by user David Stanley via Flickr.com

https://www.flickr.com/photos/davidstanleytravel/47572486101/

Page 74 Photo by user Bernard DUPONT via Flickr.com

https://www.flickr.com/photos/berniedup/34611375013/

Page 85 Photo by user Itsmatthewc via Flickr.com

https://www.flickr.com/photos/127245078@N04/15127831718

Page 91 Photo by user Anthony Sokolik via Flickr.com

https://www.flickr.com/photos/asokolik/8004675928/

Page Photo by user Bernard DUPONT via Flickr.com

https://www.flickr.com/photos/berniedup/39664785855/

References

How to Keep Red - Footed Tortoises as Pets - The Spruce Pets

https://www.thesprucepets.com/red-footed-tortoises-1237265

Red - Footed Tortoises - ReptilesMagazine.com

http://www.reptilesmagazine.com/Red-Footed-Tortoise/

Keeping and Caring for Red and Yellow - Footed Tortoises

http://www.reptilesmagazine.com/Turtles-Tortoises/Tortoise-Care/Keeping-and-Caring-for-Red-and-Yellow-Footed-Tortoises/

Basic Information Sheet: Red-Footed Tortoise - Lafeber.com

https://lafeber.com/vet/basic-information-red-footed-tortoise-chelonoidis-carbonaria/

Red - Footed Tortoise - NationalZoo.si.edu

https://nationalzoo.si.edu/animals/red-footed-tortoise

A Set - Up Guide for New Red - Foot Tortoise: Tips for Home, Health to Fun – PetSmart.com

https://www.petsmart.com/learning-center/reptile-care/a-set-up-guide-for-new-red-foot-tortoise/A0175.html

Red - Footed Tortoise - AnimalSpot.net

https://www.animalspot.net/red-footed-tortoise.html

Red Footed Tortoise - PetGuide.com

https://www.petguide.com/breeds/turtle/red-footed-tortoise/

How to Care for a Red - Footed Tortoise - HowtoCareForATortoise.com

http://www.howtocareforatortoise.com/how-to-care-for-a-red-footed-tortoise-2/

Red Footed Tortoise - Facts, Diet, Habitat & Pictures - Animalia.bio

http://animalia.bio/red-footed-tortoise

Red Footed Tortoise - Kidzone.ws

https://www.kidzone.ws/animal-facts/turtles/red-footed-tortoise.htm

Red-Foot Tortoise Care – ExoticPetVet.com

http://www.exoticpetvet.com/redfoot-tortoise-care.html

www.ingramcontent.com/pod-product-compliance
Lightning Source LLC
Chambersburg PA
CBHW060840050426
42453CB00008B/763